Contents

What are ants?

Ants are very small **insects** that you might have seen outside. Hundreds of ants live together in a group called a **colony**. Each colony makes a nest.

In the nest are a few **queen** ants, male ants and many **workers**. The queen and the male ants have wings for part of their life.

What do ants look like?

Some ants are green like the ones in the picture. Most ants are black or brown. They are the ones we are going to look at.

Ants have six legs with many **joints** and two small **claws** at the end. Ants have two eyes but they cannot see very well. They have **feelers** for touching and smelling.

How big are ants?

Big ants, like this one, are nearly half as long as your middle finger. They live in very hot countries. The black garden ants that live in **Europe** are very small.

The **queen** ant is bigger than the male ants. The **workers** are the smallest ants. They are half as big as the queen. Ants are small but very strong.

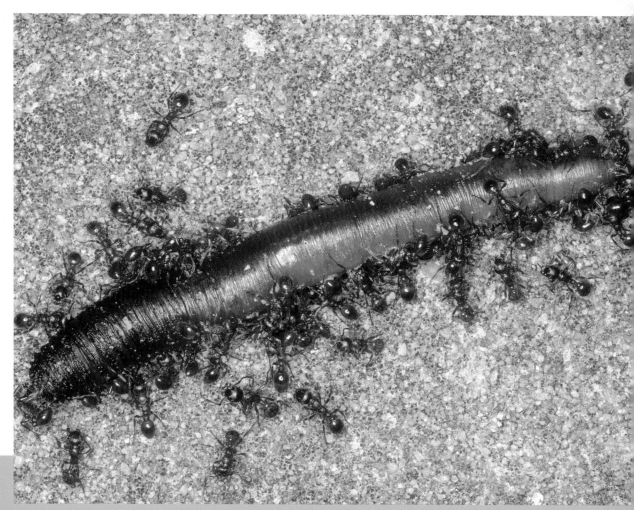

How are ants born ?

The young **queens** and male ants fly off together to **mate**. The male ants soon die and the queen ants go off to start new nests. Their wings drop off too.

The queen ant lays eggs in the soil.
When the **workers hatch** they look
after the queen ant and build the nest.

How do ants grow?

A few days after the eggs are laid, a **larva hatches** from each. After about 8 days it makes a hard **cocoon** around its body. Can you see the one cocoon?

Inside the cocoon the larva turns into a **pupa**. This takes 3 weeks. **Workers** cut open the cocoon so that the new ant can come out.

What do ants eat?

Ants like to drink **honeydew**. They get this from greenflies. The ants stroke them with their **feelers** and tiny drops of the dew come out.

Most ants like sweet things. They eat fruit and seeds or even biscuits and jam if they are left around! They also eat worms, caterpillars and other **insects**.

Which animals attack ants?

Some beetles and other **insects** eat ants. **Workers** are always on the look-out for enemies. Sometimes ants fight each other.

Birds and frogs eat some kinds of ants. Spiders eat ants if they catch them in their webs. In some countries big animals called anteaters eat ants.

Where do ants live?

Ants make their nests in places where they feel safe and warm. Some build their nests underground. Others make their nests in old logs or under stones.

Ants that live in woods put pieces of wood on top of their nests. Others use soil to keep them safe. Ants make tunnels and little rooms inside their nests.

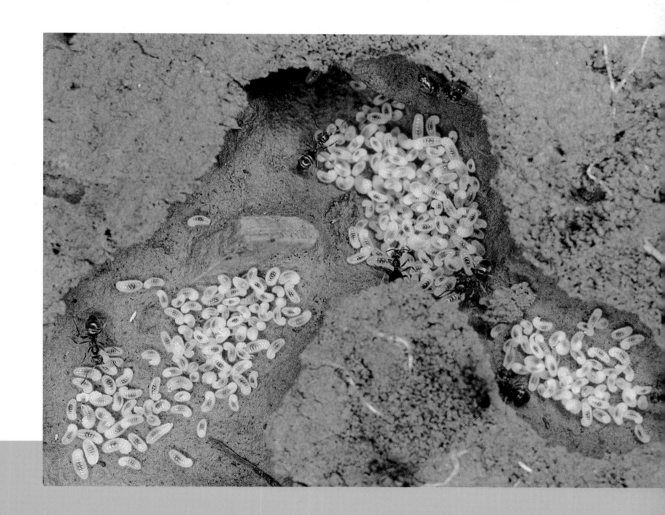

What do ants do?

When it is cold the ants sleep in their nests. When the weather is warm the **worker** ants are busy. They build the nest and keep it tidy.

The workers lick the eggs to keep them clean. They also collect food, feed the **larvae** and look after the queen and **cocoons**.

How do ants move?

Ants are very busy and so they move very quickly. They can carry big pieces of food back to the nest. Some ants follow each other in lines.

Ants use the claws on the end of their legs to help them climb. **Workers** do not fly but in the summer you might see **queen** ants and males flying.

How long do ants live?

The **queen** ant might live for 10 or 15 years. She is safe in her special room and the **workers** protect her. She has an important job to do.

The male ants live for only a few months. Their work is done when they have **mated** with the queen. The workers will live for about 5 years.

How are ants special?

Ants live and work together and help each other. Ants give off smells which other ants follow. Their **feelers** help them in many ways.

26

The ants use their feelers to tell them where they are going. Ants touch each other with their feelers. The smell tells them if an ant is a friend or an enemy.

Thinking about ants

Look at this ants' nest. Can you see the
tunnels? What jobs do you think the
ants are doing?

Here is a photograph of part of an ants' nest.

Can you say which are the **larvae** and which is the **cocoon**? Which stage comes first? What would you see when the cocoon breaks open?

Bug map

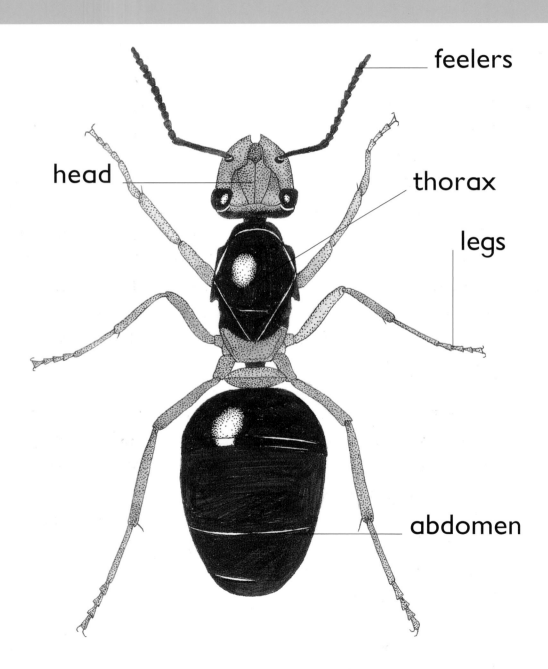

feelers

head

thorax

legs

abdomen

Glossary

claws sharp, bent points at the end of the legs. Claws are used for tearing or holding things.

cocoon the casing that grows round the larva

colony a group of insects that live together

Europe the United Kingdom, France and Spain are part of Europe

feelers two long thin tubes that stick out from the head of an insect. They may be used to feel, smell or even hear.

hatch to come out of an egg or cocoon

honeydew the sweet liquid made by greenflies

insect a small creature with six legs

joint the part of a leg where it can bend

larva (more than one = larvae) the little white grub that hatches from the egg

mate a male and female ant mate to make baby ants

pupa (more than one = pupae) older larva. The adult ant grows inside it.

queen mother ant

workers ants that do all the work

Index